WHY RABBITS EAT POOP

and Other Gross Facts about Pets

by Jody Sullivan Rake

Consultant: Tanya Dewey, PhD
University of Michigan Museum of Zoology, Ann Arbor, Michigan

CAPSTONE PRESS
a capstone imprint

First Facts is published by Capstone Press,
1710 Roe Crest Drive, North Mankato, Minnesota 56003.
www.capstonepub.com

Books published by Capstone Press are manufactured with paper
containing at least 10 percent post consumer waste.

Library of Congress Cataloging-in-Publication Data
Rake, Jody Sullivan.
  Why rabbits eat poop and other gross facts about pets / by Jody Sullivan Rake.
    p. cm.—(First facts. Gross me out.)
  Includes bibliographical references and index.
  Summary: "Describes unusual behavior of pets, including dogs, cats, rabbits, and
hermit crabs"—Provided by publisher.
  ISBN 978-1-4296-7609-0 (library binding)
  ISBN 978-1-4296-7956-5 (paperback)
  1. Pets—Behavior—Juvenile literature. I. Title.
  SF416.2.R35 2012
  636.088'7—dc23   2011035905

Editorial Credits
Lori Shores, editor; Veronica Correia, designer; Marcie Spence, media researcher;
    Kathy McColley, production specialist

Image Credits
Alamy: Myrleen Pearson, 15 (top); Shutterstock: Albert Ziganshin, 11 (bottom), Alberto
Perez Viega, 13, Anat-oli, cover (rabbit), Atovot, 5 (bottom), cath5, 7, Daniel Hilgert, 14,
dedMazay, 15 (bottom), Eric Isselee, 8, Gila R. Todd, 9, iofoto, 11 (top), Jesse Kunerth, 10,
Joshua Lewis, 4, Juriah Mosin, 21, kbrowne41, 16, Kirill Vorobyev, 6, novvy, 17 (bottom),
Oleg Kozlov, 19, Proanimus, cover (background), qingqing, 20, Regien Paassen, 5 (top),
Sergey Chirkov, 18, Steve Mann, 12, Yayayoyo, 3, 17 (top)

Printed in the United States of America in North Mankato, Minnesota.

102011   006405CGS12

TABLE OF CONTENTS

That's So Gross!

Pets bring joy to our lives as members of our families. But sometimes pets do some pretty gross things. Come and explore some of the pet world's yuckiest behaviors. Get ready to be grossed out!

Rabbits Eat What?

Cute, fluffy rabbits have an icky habit. They eat poop! Rabbits eat a lot of greens, such as grass and leafy weeds. But those greens don't break down as easily as other foods. Many **nutrients** pass through a rabbit's body without being used. When rabbits eat their poop, they get the nutrients they missed the first time.

nutrient—parts of food, like vitamins, that are used for growth

Gross Fact!

Rabbits produce two types of poop. They eat the small soft droppings, but the larger dry ones are left behind.

The Cat Threw Up... Again!

Ewww, the cat threw up a gooey, hairy mess. What's going on? Cats swallow a lot of fur. That's because they use their tongues to clean themselves. That swallowed fur sometimes forms a lump in a cat's stomach. The cat throws up to get rid of the hair ball.

My Ferret Plays in its Litter Box!

Did you know litter boxes are just as fun as sandboxes? Well, for ferrets they are. In the wild, ferrets hunt by digging into other animals' **burrows**. Pet ferrets don't hunt, but they still have an **instinct** to dig. Sometimes the only place they can dig is their own litter box. Gross!

burrow—a tunnel or hole in the ground made or used by an animal
instinct—behavior that is natural rather than learned

What's That Dog Doing?

Scoot, scoot. There goes the dog, dragging its butt on the carpet. It looks funny and gross, but it serves a purpose. Dogs have **glands** that make a stinky liquid. When they poop, the liquid drips out to mark their **territory**. Sometimes the glands get too full. The dog rubs its rear end on the ground to empty the glands.

gland—an organ in the body that makes natural chemicals and helps those chemicals leave the body

territory—an area of land that an animal claims as its own to live in

Gross Fact!

Ever see a guinea pig do this? They have scent glands too.

Pee-ew! The Cat is Spraying Pee!

Cats have a stinky way of sharing information. They get the inside scoop from smelling each other's urine. Cats spray pee to mark their territory. The smell also tells other cats they're ready to **mate**. It's too bad they have to spray their news all over the house!

mate—to join together to produce young

What Happened to My Lizard's Tail?

Some lizards can do an amazing thing. When in danger, a lizard squeezes its muscles and breaks off its tail. The **predator** grabs the tail, and the lizard gets away. Pet lizards sometimes drop their tails if they are startled. The tail continues to wiggle for several minutes!

predator—an animal that hunts other animals for food

Gross Fact!

Don't worry about the lizard.
Most lizards grow their tails
back in a few weeks or months.

15

That Dog Must Be Crazy!

Dogs look cute when they roll around. But sometimes they roll around on stinky things. And they do it on purpose! Their sense of smell is different from ours. What smells bad to us may smell great to dogs. The opposite is also true. After a bath, some dogs roll on gross stuff to cover the soap smell!

Gross Fact!

This smelly behavior may also go back to wild dogs and wolves. Before hunting, wolves roll around on a dead deer to cover their own smell.

Buggy Rat Eyes!

Big, buggy rat eyes sometimes get even buggier! Rats grind their teeth to keep them sharp for chewing. The same muscles that work their jaws also push on their eyes. So when rats grind their teeth, their eyes bulge in and out!

There Were Two—Now There's One

Some hermit crabs will eat a newly **molted** friend. When hermit crabs molt, their bodies are soft. They could be in danger if a hungry hermit crab comes along. Do your hermit crabs a favor. Keep them separated when it's time to molt!

molt—to shed an outer layer of skin

GLOSSARY

burrow (BUHR-oh)—a tunnel or hole in the ground made or used by an animal

gland (GLAND)—an organ in the body that makes natural chemicals and helps those chemicals leave the body

instinct (IN-stingkt)—behavior that is natural rather than learned

mate (MATE)—to join together to produce young

molt (MOHLT)—to shed an outer layer of skin

nutrient (NOO-tree-uhnt)—parts of food, like vitamins, that are used for growth

predator (PRED-uh-tur)—an animal that hunts other animals for food

territory (TER-uh-tor-ee)—an area of land that an animal claims as its own to live in

READ MORE

Hanna, Jack. *The Wackiest, Wildest, Weirdest Animals in the World.* Nashville: Thomas Nelson, 2009.

Polydoros, Lori. *Strange but True Animals.* Strange but True. Mankato, Minn.: Capstone Press, 2011.

Slade, Suzanne. *Why Do Dogs Drool?: And Other Questions Kids Have About Dogs.* Kids' Questions. Minneapolis: Picture Window Books, 2010.

INTERNET SITES

FactHound offers a safe, fun way to find Internet sites related to this book. All of the sites on FactHound have been researched by our staff.

Here's all you do:

Visit *www.facthound.com*

Type in this code: 9781429676090

 Check out projects, games and lots more at
www.capstonekids.com

INDEX